Māui

THE MISCHIEF MAKER

AS TOLD AND ILLUSTRATED
BY DIETRICH VAREZ

EDITED BY LILIKALĀ KAMEʻELEIHIWA

BISHOP MUSEUM PRESS, 1991

Native Hawaiian Culture and Arts Program

Ua lehulehu a manomano ka ʻikena a ka Hawaiʻi.
Great and numerous is the knowledge of the Hawaiians.
ʻŌlelo Noʻeau 2814

The reprinting of this publication is sponsored by the Native Hawaiian Culture and Arts Program in celebration of the Legacy of Excellence of Native Hawaiian culture. The Legacy of Excellence volumes are devoted to generating an appreciation of Native Hawaiian traditions, art, and language through education, awareness, and recognition of excellence in Native Hawaiian achievement.

The views and conclusions contained in this document are those of the authors and should not be interpreted as representing the opinions or policies of the U.S. Government. Mention of trade names or commercial products does not constitute their endorsement by the U.S. Government.

Bishop Museum Press
1525 Bernice Street
Honolulu, Hawaiʻi 96817
www.bishopmuseum.org/press

Library of Congress Catalog Card No. 91-072830

ISBN-13: 978-0-930897-53-6
ISBN-10: 0-930897-53-6

Printed in China

Hawaiians and their Polynesian cousins—Maoris, Tahitians, and Cook Islanders—have told stories about Māui for a very long time. Each island group has its own stories. Sometimes one island will have more than one version, each coming from a different place. In Hawai'i, there are several different versions of the Māui stories.

On the island of Māui, for instance, there is a West Māui version as well as an East Māui version. A series of Māui stories comes from the island of Lāna'i, another from Hilo, on Hawai'i, as well as one from Kaua'i and another from Wai'anae, on O'ahu. Once there must have been many more. Because the story is told in so many places, we can tell that it is very old, and that Māui was probably once part of the myths about some of the oldest of the Polynesian Gods, Kāne and Kanaloa, the Gods of life and death.

The Polynesians took the stories with them each time they sailed to new islands, and in time the stories changed and became part of the place where they were being told. That is why it is important to keep the different Māui stories separate. Each small detail belongs to a different place and people and this is how we remember them.

This telling of the Māui stories is largely Hawaiian, mostly from the islands of Māui and O'ahu, and is based on the Kumulipo, the ancient creation chant of the Hawaiians that tells how the world and everything in it was made. (The source of each Māui episode is given in the Notes section at the end of this book.) In Tahiti and Aotearoa (New Zealand), Māui was what Hawaiians call a *kupua,* a being who had the *mana,* or power, to change his body into many different forms. In his adventures, Māui learned to control the elements of the world—the sea, the sky, the sun—and everything that lived in it. He could take many different shapes. Because he would use his shapes to trick others, he was called Māui-akamai, or Māui the Clever One.

In Hawai'i, Māui was a *keiki 'eu,* a rascal-child, who was always getting into mischief and uncovering people's secrets. He was disobedient, and sometimes his tricks made the Gods, the *Akua,* very angry. Most of the stories about Māui's death agree that if Māui did die, he was killed by the Gods for being such a troublemaker. But Māui was a trickster and a shape-changer. Some say he may still be with us.

Māui's mother was Hina-a-keahi, Hina of the Fire. Her cousins were the *'alae* birds, who knew the secret of making fire.

Māui's father was Akalana. At the time of this story, Hina-a-keahi and Akalana already had three sons, whose names all began with Māui. They were Māui-mua (Māui the first), Māui-waena (Māui the middle one), and Māui-iki-iki (Māui the little one).

One day Hina went to the seashore to pick *limu,* or seaweed. There, at the edge of the water, she found a *malo*, a man's loincloth. She put it on and fell asleep.

Some time later, she woke and learned that the *malo* belonged to her husband, Akalana, and that she had mysteriously become pregnant after putting it on.

When Akalana heard this, he said, "This child will be our *aliʻi*! He will be our chief." Māui-akamai would become the most famous of all his brothers.

Even before he was born, Māui-akamai liked to play tricks. He would escape from his mother's womb and run along the sea-cliffs, teasing the fishermen. When they grew angry and chased him, he would sneak back inside his mother, where they could not find him.

But Māui was so eager to see the world that he didn't wait nine months to be born, like ordinary children. He was born early, and began his adventures right away.

Māui was not an easy child. He disobeyed his parents. He could never sit still and do as he was told. He was always playing tricks on his brothers. His parents, Hina and Akalana, didn't know what to do with him.

Finally, at her wits' end, Hina cut off some of her long hair and wrapped Māui in it. She took him down to the edge of the ocean and set him adrift.

Māui-akamai floated out to sea. His adventures had begun.

As Māui floated in the ocean, a large jellyfish swam up under him and carried him far away to the sacred lands of Kuaihelani where the great *Akua*, the Gods Kāne and Kanaloa, lived. On this long journey the birds and the fish were Māui's companions.

Māui stayed in Kuaihelani for some time, living with the Gods and learning their ways.

While Māui-akamai was living with Kāne and Kanaloa in Kuaihelani, he learned about many things. One of them was *'awa,* the Gods' favorite drink. It was made from the leaves of the black-stemmed *'awa* bush, and the *Akua* drank it from their huge *kānoa* bowl. They liked *'awa* because it made them feel happy, and also because it was good medicine. Kāne liked *'awa* so much that he chose it as one of his *kinolau,* or body forms. When he wanted to, he could become the *'awa* plant.

Māui decided that one day he would steal the *'awa* plant from Kāne and Kanaloa, and take it back to the world of his people.

Kāne and Kanaloa grew another useful plant in Kuaihelani. It was called *'ohe*, or bamboo, and sometimes Kāne liked to live in it, too. Its trunk was long and hollow with joints in it. Its leaves were green, sharp, and hairy.

Māui bent one stalk all the way to the ground, but it didn't break. He learned that *'ohe* was very useful for making fishing poles, carrying drinking water, and building houses. Very sharp knives could also be made from it by splitting the trunk.

Māui decided to take the *'ohe* home with him along with the *'awa*. He would give them to his mother, Hina-a-keahi, to plant by her doorway.

As time passed, Māui grew restless in Kuaihelani, and at last the day came when he knew he must return to his home and his people. When he left, he took *'awa* and *'ohe* plants with him as gifts.

When he reached his home, two of his mother's brothers were standing like posts by her doorway. They refused to let him pass. Their names were Kia-loa, Long Post, and Kia-a-kapoko, Short Post. In a fierce fight, Māui uprooted them both and threw them to the ground. Blood poured from his forehead, but he had won, and the entrance to his mother's house was clear.

One day Māui's mother wanted to eat fish, and so, to please her, Māui decided he would learn to catch fish. Hina sent him to his father, who gave him the sacred fishhook named Manai-a-kalani, or Hook from the Heavens. It was curved, with a sharp barb on the end that made it very hard for the fish to wriggle off once it was caught.

The fish that Māui wanted to catch was a giant *ulua* fish named Pīmoe. He lived deep in the ocean, and Hina told Māui there was only one way to catch him. She said Māui must use Pīmoe's bird-sister, the *'alae* bird, as bait, for only the *'alae* could bring Pīmoe up out of the deep.

Pīmoe was not an ordinary fish. He could turn himself into an island whenever he wanted to. When he did this he became very, very heavy. Māui wanted to catch Pīmoe so that he could join the islands together and make one large island.

Māui told his brothers to paddle far out to sea, to the deepest spot, where he knew Pīmoe lived. After many days they found the place. Māui let down his hook, Manai-a-kalani, with the *'alae* bird on it as bait. Down, down it went, to the bottom of the sea. Pīmoe swallowed it and began to pull on the line.

For two days and nights Māui fought to bring the great fish up from the bottom. His brothers struggled to keep their canoe from overturning. The waves churned and the ocean heaved with the fierce battle.

The struggle went on for a long time. Māui told his brothers, "Whatever you do, don't look at Pīmoe. Just keep paddling." He was careful not to look at the giant fish himself.

Finally Māui's brothers caught sight of shore and thought they were safe. They looked back at Pīmoe, struggling beneath them, and at that moment the line broke and the great *ulua* died and became solid land that would move no more. That is how Māui brought land from the bottom of the sea and that is why the islands were never united.

Having fished an island out of the sea, Māui jumped out of the canoe and began to free the sacred hook from the island. When he had freed the great hook, he threw it up into the sky, where it became the constellation known as Māui's Fish-hook. It still hangs there today, known to some as Scorpio.

Before Māui, the earth was a strange place. The sky lay right down along the ground, and so there was very little room for anything. Trees could not grow very far. Their leaves had to grow flat, as they still do today. Birds had no room to fly. And worst of all, people couldn't stand up and walk. They were forced to crawl on their hands and knees through the low bushes.

The people had heard of Māui's great strength and his extraordinary powers. They came to him, complaining about the low sky. "Please help us," they said. "Please lift the sky."

This was just the kind of challenge Māui enjoyed. Just then, a woman came by, carrying a gourd full of water. Māui felt thirsty and asked her for a drink, and in return he promised to lift the sky for her.

After he had drunk the woman's water, Māui began to push the sky with all his might. Soon he had lifted it to the tops of the trees. He kept pushing until he had lifted the sky to the top of Ka'uiki Hill, in Hāna, Māui. Then he braced himself, gave one last push, and lifted the sky to where it still is, above the great volcano Haleakalā. Today, the sky may hang low over Haleakalā, but it never touches Ka'uiki Hill.

Māui's mother, Hina-a-keahi, made fine clothes for him out of *kapa* a cloth made by pounding the bark of the *wauke* tree. After it has been soaked and pounded, *kapa* must dry in the sun before it can be worn.

But in those times the days were very short, because the sun would always race across the sky. The people barely had enough daylight to do their work before the sun was gone and it was time to sleep again. Hina's *kapa* never had time to dry in the sun. She asked Māui to do something about it.

Hina-a-keahi told Māui to ask his grandmother, Mahuie, how to catch the sun. Mahuie lived on Mount Haleakalā, the great volcano whose name means "House of the Sun."

Near the top was the house of his old, nearly blind grandmother. Each morning her rooster crowed to tell her when the sun came up. And each morning she roasted bananas for the sun.

Māui began the long steep climb up Haleakalā, where the sun lived.

When Māui got to his grandmother's house, he asked her how he could catch Kalā, the sun. Mahuie gave Māui a sacred adze and a strong rope. She told him to hide in the roots of the old *wiliwili* tree that grew near her house, and to lasso Kalā's legs as soon as he appeared on the eastern rim of the crater.

Māui hid in the roots of the tree, as Mahuie told him to. Soon the rooster crowed, and Māui could see the sun creeping over the edge of the mountains to begin its race across the sky.

Māui leapt from his hiding place and quickly threw his rope over the sun. The battle had begun.

Māui did just what his grandmother had told him to, and soon Kalā was caught in his ropes and struggling to escape back into the sea. Using Mahuie's rope, Māui tied the sun to the roots of the *wiliwili* tree.

Once he had tied Kalā, Māui began to beat him with his adze. To punish him for not giving the people enough light, Māui broke some of Kalā's strongest legs, leaving him only his weakest ones. Now the sun would have to crawl across the sky. Kalā begged Māui to stop, and promised never again to hurry.

From then on the days were much longer, so that Hina-a-keahi and all the others could dry their *kapa* in the sun, and the people could have fine clothes to wear.

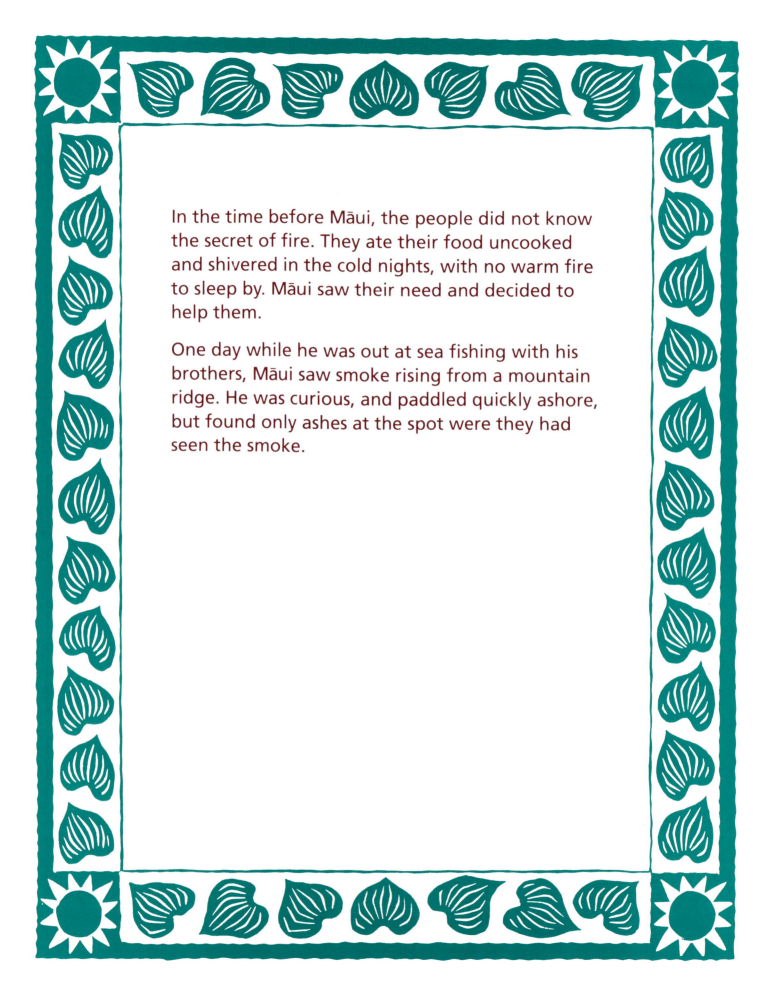

In the time before Māui, the people did not know the secret of fire. They ate their food uncooked and shivered in the cold nights, with no warm fire to sleep by. Māui saw their need and decided to help them.

One day while he was out at sea fishing with his brothers, Māui saw smoke rising from a mountain ridge. He was curious, and paddled quickly ashore, but found only ashes at the spot were they had seen the smoke.

This happened several times. Each time they found only ashes. Finally Māui decided to trick the fire-makers. He hid behind a rock and sent his brothers to sea in the canoe with a large *kapa*-covered gourd that from far away looked just like him.

The trick worked. From his hiding place, Māui watched a large group of *'alae* birds gather, make a fire, and perch around it, roasting bananas. These *'alae* birds were the fire-makers, and they were the cousins of Hina-a-keahi, his mother. He watched and listened. The *'alae* birds didn't want to share their secret with anyone, not even with their own cousin's son. That was why they always waited until Māui went out fishing before making their fires.

But Māui must have made a sound, because the birds saw him and took fright. Quickly, they put out the fire and ran off into the bushes.

Māui chased after them and caught their leader, ʻAlaehuapī, or ʻAlae the Stingy, who was so full of roasted bananas that she couldn't run very fast. Māui forced ʻAlaehuapī to teach him the art of making fire. At first she tried to trick him by telling him to rub together the stalks of the banana and also the taro plants. But those plants were full of water and wouldn't make a spark. Māui was very angry, and threatened to kill her unless she told him how to make fire.

Then ʻAlaehuapī tried to fool Māui again. She told him that fire was hidden in green wood. Māui found that this didn't work either, but he didn't give up. He became angry and tried to choke ʻAlaehuapī, and at last she told Māui the right kind of wood to use, and what to do with it. Once he had learned the secret of fire-making, Māui punished ʻAlaehuapī by rubbing a red spot on her forehead, which she has to this day.

Māui invented the first kite and was very fond of kite flying. His kites were bigger than a house and shaped like the *lupe,* or stingray, and the kite string was made of the strongest *'olonā* cord.

When he tried out his first kite, Māui prayed for *mana*, for power for his kite and string. The huge kite began to rise very slowly, but there was not enough wind to carry it all the way up.

Then Māui remembered Kaleiiokū, an old *kahuna*, or priest, who lived far back in Waipi'o valley on the island of Hawai'i. This green valley was known for its winds and rains, as well as for its taro paddies, or *lo'i*.

Kaleiiokū had a covered calabash in which he kept the winds. Whenever he wanted to, he could open the *ipu-makani,* or wind-gourd, and let out winds and storms.

Māui went to Waipi'o valley and asked Kaleiiokū to give him a wind to fly his kite. The old *kahuna* agreed, and when he opened his gourd, out rushed a gust of wind that carried Māui's kite far up into the sky, where it floated gracefully, like a stingray gliding through the sea. After that, Māui always had enough wind for his kite.

Māui passed on his love of kite flying to his people, who still fly kites today.

In time, Māui married a woman named Kumulama from Waiʻanae, on the island of Oʻahu. One day, after he had gone out fishing, he brought back two fish, a *moi* and an *ulua.* He took them to Luaʻehu Heiau to offer them to the Gods in thanks for his good luck, but, feeling hungry, he began to eat one of the fish, even though he knew he shouldn't.

Just then Māui saw Peʻapeʻa Makawalu, a giant bat with eight eyes, swoop down, snatch up his wife Kumulama, and fly off with her. Māui dropped the fish and tried to follow them in his canoe, but he couldn't keep up with Peʻapeʻa.

Māui did not know where the bat had taken his wife, so he asked his mother, Hina-a-keahi, what to do. She sent him to his grandfather, Kū'olokele, for advice.

Kū'olokele was a hunchback. He lived at Keahumoa in Waipahū, on the island of O'ahu. Māui went to see him, and quickly straightened Kū'olokele's back by hitting it with a rock. His grandfather was so grateful that he promised Māui he would help him find his wife.

Using feathers, ti leaves, *'ie'ie*, and *'olonā* cord, Kū'olokele showed Māui how to build a giant bird kite. When it was finished, they tested it from a high mountain slope. It worked perfectly. With his kite, Māui could now follow the giant bat and rescue Kumulama.

Kū'olokele told Māui that Pe'ape'a was an *ali'i,* or chief, of the island of Kaua'i. Then he told him what he must do next. Māui thanked his grandfather and flew off after Pe'ape'a.

Māui followed his grandfather's instructions and flew to Mānā, a place on Kaua'i where Pe'ape'a lived. When he heard about the strange bird, Pe'ape'a said to the people there, "That is my bird. It is *kapu.* It is only for me, and I will protect it." When Māui landed, the people led him to the sleeping house of their chief.

In the sleeping house, Māui waited for night to come and the bat to fall asleep. But Pe'ape'a had eight eyes, and kept two of them open while the rest slept.

When morning had almost come Māui still had not had a chance to kill Pe'ape'a, so he prayed to his mother to hold back the dawn. Finally, all of the bat's eyes were closed. Māui swiftly climbed out of his bird-body and cut off the great bat's head, taking out the eyes. He found Kumulama, and together they flew home in the bird kite. When they got there, Māui drank the eyes of Pe'ape'a in a cup of *'awa.* He had destroyed the giant bat and rescued his wife.

One day Māui's mother, Hina-a-keahi, went to live in a cave by the Wailuku River in Hilo, on the island of Hawai'i. In the river there were many pools formed by lava rocks. The water rushed through the pools so fast that it seemed at times to be boiling. At night, Hina would come out of her cave to sit by the pools and watch the moon shining in the water.

The Wailuku River was also the home of a giant eel named Kuna. Kuna wanted Hina to be his wife and come live with him in the river, but Hina refused, and Kuna became very angry. First he tried to drive Hina out of her cave by stopping up the water in the river. Then he threw logs and large stones into the water. Finally, Kuna flooded Hina's cave by making the river rise and overflow its banks, nearly drowning Hina. From her cave, she called to Māui to help her.

Māui heard Hina's calls and rushed to help her. But Kuna saw Māui coming, and hid in the river pools. Māui wasn't fooled. He heated stones in a fire and threw them into the pools, making them steam and boil until Kuna had to come out. Then Māui chased the giant eel from pool to pool, until finally he trapped him and killed him with a wooden club. Māui had saved his mother.

There are many stories of Māui's death. One takes place in Waipi'o Valley on the island of Hawai'i, where the Gods Kāne and Kanaloa lived. Māui spotted the Gods cooking one day and tried to steal their bananas by spearing them with a sharp stick. Kanaloa flew into a rage, chased Māui down and dashed his brains out on the rocks. It is said that the earth of Waipi'o Valley is stained red with Māui's blood.

The Maori of Aotearoa tell another story. They say Māui wanted to conquer the Goddess of death, Hine-nui-te-po, so that people could live forever. Māui's mother told him that if he traveled through the body of Hine-nui-te-po and came out of her mouth, she would lose the power of death over humans. So Māui turned himself into a caterpillar and crawled into her womb.

Māui had brought his bird brothers along and told them they must be absolutely silent, as Hine-nui-te-po was sleeping. But his bird brothers couldn't resist giggling at the sight, and their laughter woke up the Goddess. Furious, she crushed Māui to death.

We cannot be sure of what really happened to Māui, or even that he is really dead. After all, according to some, he was a *kupua,* a shape-changer, and could thus take any form he wanted. It may be that Māui has simply gone off on another adventure in another part of Polynesia, and will soon reappear. Māui-akamai may be laughing at us now, wherever he is.

Notes on the origin of the Māui stories as they appear in this book

Māui's family: This version is from the Kumulipo, the ancient Hawaiian creation chant.

Māui's conception: A Hawaiian version, from Hāna, East Māui, which is an important source of Māui stories.

Māui's prenatal adventures: A Hawaiian version, from Lāhaina, West Māui.

Māui's early birth: A Maori version.

Māui as a difficult child: The Hawaiian and Maori versions agree here.

Māui is set adrift: This is the Maori version; in the Hawaiian versions, the parents are often exasperated with Māui, but do not abandon him.

Māui and the jellyfish: This comes from the Maori version, in which Māui is taken to the land of the gods. However, the place name Kuaihelani is Hawaiian, and appears in traditional stories about Kāne and Kanaloa. In this book, Māui's adventures with Kāne and Kanaloa are from the Kumulipo. Thus the story merges Hawaiian and Maori versions.

Māui steals the *'awa* plant: This part of the story is Hawaiian, mentioned in the Kumulipo and other traditional Kāne stories.

Māui takes the *'ohe* home to Hina-a-keahi: A Hawaiian version, from the Kumulipo.

Māui uproots Kia: A Hawaiian version, from the Kumulipo.

Māui and the fishhook, Manai-a-kalani: A Hawaiian version, from the Kumulipo.

Māui sets off to catch Pīmoe: This part of the story is Hawaiian, from the Kumulipo, and is also told on Kaua'i and in Wai'anae, O'ahu. (Note: the illustration here shows Māui's brothers fishing with him, but the Hawaiian story actually speaks of only Māui fishing.)

Māui battles Pīmoe: A Hawaiian version, from the Kumulipo, and also told in Hāna, Māui, and in Wai'anae, O'ahu.

Pīmoe turns into an island: There are three Hawaiian versions of this. One is from Wai'anae, O'ahu, in which the island is Kaua'i; another is from Hāna, Māui, and the third is from Hilo, Hawai'i, in which the island was Mokuola, or Coconut Island, in Hilo Bay.

Manai-a-kalani becomes a constellation: This version is from the Cook Islands.

Māui lifts up the sky: A Hawaiian version.

Māui lassos the sun: This version is Hawaiian, from Hāna, Māui.

Māui learns the secret of fire from the *'alae* birds: This version is Hawaiian, from Hāna, or from nearby Kaupō, East Māui. In Polynesia, family relationships were very strong, and it was a serious offense for a family member to refuse to give something to a relation who asked for it. This is why Māui was so angry with 'Alaehuapī, and punished her so severely.

Māui invents the kite: This part of the story is Hawaiian.

Pe'ape'a steals Kumulama: This version is Hawaiian, from Wai'anae, O'ahu.

Hina and the giant eel, Kuna: This version is Hawaiian, from Hilo, Hawai'i.

Kanaloa kills Māui in Waipi'o: This version is Hawaiian, from Wai'anae, O'ahu. (The Kumulipo version tells of Māui's death, presumably of old age, at Hakiupu'u, O'ahu.)

Designed by Barbara Pope